HELP!
I'm in College

HELP!
I'm in College

Roy G. Gesch

Publishing House
St. Louis

Other Books by Roy G. Gesch

On Active Duty
A Husband Prays
A Wife Prays
God's World Through Young Eyes
Lord of the Young Crowd
Discover Europe (coauthor Dorothy Gesch)

Concordia Publishing House, St. Louis, Missouri
Copyright © 1969 Concordia Publishing House
Revised Version © 1976 Concordia Publishing House

MANUFACTURED IN THE UNITED STATES OF AMERICA

Library of Congress Cataloging in Publication Data
Gesch, Roy G
    Help! I'm in college!

    1. College students—Prayer-books and devotions—
English. I. Title.
BV4850.G4 1976   242'.6'3   76-52470
ISBN 0-570-03100-1

11 12 13 14 15 16 17 18 19 20   CB   89 88 87 86 85 84 83 82 81 80

To Gary and Karen,
as they trade in cap and gown
for their new roles in life

Contents

Preface

Everybody knows college is not all homecomings and pep rallies, dates and parties.

Nor is it all an automatic routine of lectures, library, and study hours.

It's a time of learning to think for oneself; a time of being confronted with the good and bad of the world of thought; a time of learning to evaluate and then take a stand on the basis of personal judgment.

It's a time to appreciate freedom without taking liberties; a time to dare to be different without becoming offensively rebellious.

It's also a time to deepen your personal acquaintance with your loving God; a time for faith to become strong conviction; a time to prove your courage by not being a coward about Christ.

You're on your own in college. Yet happily that's not quite true. He who loves you most of all promised, "I am with you always!" I hope the words in this book help you know Him better.

An ancient Greek philosopher observed, "All things flow." Time and human tides effect flow and change on campus too.

In these last few years world events and conditions have greatly altered the contemporary scene. As usual, the college campus is the first testing ground for new reactions and ideas.

Yet God's assurances and promises have not changed. They are as timely and significant to you, the student of the latter seventies, as they have been to those who walked this way before.

God is with you. Go forward confidently in His love.

Roy G. Gesch

Spare Me a Moment, Lord?

Could You give me, Father,
  a few moments of Your time?
I have quite a few things on my mind,
and I feel very much the need
  of talking them over —
    especially with You.

It used to be
  that I could go to my folks.
We'd work things over together.
Though sometimes we'd end up
  feeling we hadn't really
    understood each other,
they were usually
  quite a bit of help to me.
    More than I would let on.
I really miss that now
  when we're not together as much.

Oh, there's plenty of opportunity
  to talk things over around here.

There are rap sessions
   at any hour
   of any day or night.
You can walk in almost any door,
   and someone's glad
      to throw books aside
      and talk awhile.
But it's not the same.

Everything's too one-sided around here.
They have the same problems,
   the same questions I have —
      many even worse.
But some aren't looking for answers.
They're perfectly content
   to settle for no solution,
to accept the question
   as the final word.

Lord, I can't!
   I have to go farther,
      delve deeper!
That's why I'm turning to You.
   I'm so grateful I can!
That's why I'm asking for a little
   of Your time and patience
      and for Your guidance.

Yet even as I ask for Your time,
   I'm aware that
You are with me always,
   just as You promised.
I'm the one that doesn't take the time
   to be with You.
Forgive me for treating You as last resort,
   and help me keep in touch.

Let me also say, Father,
   it's good to have You around.
We need You pretty badly
   here on campus.
Give me sense and faith enough
   to keep turning to You
      and listening to You
   and going it Your way.
Keep me close to You
   all through my college years.

Why Am I Here?

First off, Father, I'd like to rethink
   what I'm doing in college.
Sometimes I'm not so sure
   I'm here for the right reason.

It used to be that going to college
   was the line of least resistance.
It was the thing to do
   and the place to be
      when you're my age.

Just putting in the time
   and getting the degree
seemed to be the automatic assurance
   of getting a good job,
   of having the edge in competition.
They used to say
   no matter what courses you took,
   no matter what grades you got,
as long as you had that piece of paper
   you had it made.

If it ever was that way,
   I don't see it that way now.
The rising rate of unemployment
   and the general recession
make that pretty unlikely today.

I know there are both guys and gals
   who have the ability to qualify,
   who are doing reasonably good work,
but who still haven't found the point
   or purpose in being here.
But they're going along,
   keeping their folks happy,
hoping they will find themselves.

There are also those who look on college
   as a necessary evil,
the sin qua non with which they'll contend
   to guarantee a higher income.

And there are a few who regard it
   as a high-class matrimonial bureau.
They're mostly concerned
   about finding someone
who will enable them to live
   on the level they would like
      to become accustomed to.

I know it's hard to catch proper perspective
    when you're in the middle of the picture.
And I know goals and attitudes change
    as months and semesters pass.
But Father, I pray for them and me:
Make us wise and mature enough
    to recognize and appreciate this
    as the opportunity
        it really is.

There is so much to learn
    that can benefit us for life.
Even the art of how to learn is a plus
    that can be gained here and now.
This is the time and this the place
    to get the knowledge
        and understanding,
to become trained and equipped
    for what lies ahead.

Make me eager
    to get out of these years
        whatever I can.
Let me soak up
        whatever facts and skills
are necessary for a full
        and meaningful life.

And don't let me neglect
   spiritual growth.
You said, "The fear of the Lord
   is the beginning of wisdom."
Man has problems when he has
a stunted mind
   or a neglected body.
It's even worse when he has
   a neglected soul.
Health and strength of body and mind
   cannot compensate
      for being spiritually dead inside,
   for having all the lights turned off
      where You are concerned.

Keep me ready to learn of You,
   for only then will I have the balance
      and perspective of true wisdom.

Who Am I, Lord?

As I shuffle from building to building
  and pass hundreds of other students
    day after day,
with seldom a smile or nod
  or word of greeting,
I tend at times, Father,
  to feel a little lost in the crowd.

Before you hit the campus,
  you have a momentary
    delusion of grandeur.
"I'm going to college!" you say,
  and you feel pretty important.
Relatives and friends treat you
  as if it were a really big deal.
And it is.

Until you're here!

Now who am I, Lord?
  Am I less than I was before?

19

It's rather deflating to be reminded
    that chemically I have little value.
The suggestion that I may be a primate,
    a little more highly developed
        than most apes,
    offers no sense of worth.
The historic reality that
    probably only one of 10,000,000
accomplishes anything worthwhile enough
    to cause him to be remembered
        by generations to come
does not generate much enthusiasm
    for making something out of life.
Ditto for philosophy.
    Psychology doesn't help much either.

Funny, isn't it, Father,
    that in this day,
when science is really enabling man
    to attain great heights,
the idea of true human dignity and worth
    is upheld primarily in Your Word.

Perhaps now more than ever
    I treasure the glorious truth
that You deemed me worth saving
    and claiming as Your child.

I guess deep down inside
   what we all long for most
      is love.

When One cares enough
   to give the very best,
we know we've found such love.
That's what You did in sending Jesus
   to be our Savior
and what Jesus did in dying
   for our eternal good.

Father, let me never regard
   the gift of love lightly —
whether Yours for me,
   or my parents' and friends'.
If I can keep that love in mind,
   Yours and theirs,
and remember whose I am,
   I have all the incentive I need
to lay hold on life enthusiastically
   and make the most of it.
It's then I know
   that my life is really important,
   that I do have true and lasting worth.

And Who Are They?

The thought just hit me, Father,
    that the other human pieces
        on the campus chessboard
    are not much different from me.

Yes, there are apparent differences—
    in race,
    in background,
    in manners and morals,
    in attire and appearance,
    in attitudes and ideals.
But deep down inside,
    are they very different?

If I sense basic needs,
    so do they.
If I have conflict and question,
    so do they.
If I am caught in a tangle
    of ambitions and frustrations,
        so are they.

But recognizing this does not tell me
   who they are
or how I should relate to them.

Relate we must,
      for we are not inanimate blocks
         rattling in an academic box.
Inevitably we affect each other
   as our lives touch.
But how?

Am I to be a plastic mass,
   with no particular design of my own,
to be shaped and sized
   by the pressure of this peer group?

Or am I to be like yeast in the dough
   (the way Jesus put it),
working quietly and pervasively
   to make the whole more palatable?

Shall I surrender
      principles and convictions
   to one with stronger voice
      and greater following?
Or do I stand on principle and conviction
   and pray that others be encouraged
      to do likewise?

Lord, I know what I must do.
  Give me the courage to do it!

And as I relate properly,
  help me to see all these others
as those for whom, like me,
  You planned an eternal destiny.

It's obvious that some have disclaimed
  Your parental tie.
They won't admit to any relationship
  with You at all.
It's also apparent that there are those
  who count it high honor
    to be recognized as Yours.
Just let me remember
  which side of the fence I'm on.

I fear, Father,
  that I'm not going to like them all.
In fact, there are some
  I rather dislike already.
Regardless, keep me mindful
  of Your loving concern for them,
and show me how to love them Your way.

Where Am I Going?

Where am I going, Lord?

Up to this point my path
   has been singularly clear
      and straight.
But I can see that
   not very far ahead
it branches out bewilderingly
   in many directions.
Which way is mine, Lord?
   How can I be sure?

What if I make a mistake?
Many older people claim they did.
They say wistfully:
   "I wish I were your age again.
      I'd do things differently."
Would they really?
   Or are they just making small talk?
Is this just another case
   of the greener grass elsewhere?

It seems to me
  they must have set their course
    knowledgeably and determinedly,
at least on the basis
  of standards that prevailed,
    standards they accepted.
There must have been a time when they
  excitedly accepted the challenge
    of rat-race competition,
when they willfully encumbered
    themselves
  with mortgages and payments,
when they desired above all
  to settle into a comfortable routine.
Now they wish they had done differently?
  It doesn't make sense.
Then why don't they
  do something about it?
Does one ever really reach a point
  where he can no longer change his way?
It would seem to me
  that the door is always open
    to higher goals,
    to a better life —
unless one lacks the courage
  or the faith to make a change.

So, Lord, don't let me carry weights
   that are unnecessarily heavy.
Give me the peace of realizing
   that my immediate decisions
do not have to affect my whole life.
 And show me the way, Lord.
   No, better yet—
"Teach me Thy way, O Lord,
   and lead me in a plain path."

Fill me with such ideals,
   and give me such a sense of values
that I may not make the mistakes
   others claim they made
      and probably did.

Keep me mindful that there are
   greater objectives
      and sweeter rewards
than those the establishment
   seems to hold so high.
The top of the totem pole
   is a lonely place.
Material gains instill
   a sick fear of material loss.
Money has real worth only as long
   as there is awareness of need.

Lord, do not let these common goals
  warp my sense of judgment.
Help me to see life
  as You intended it to be,
so I don't try to gain the whole world
  and yet lose real life itself.
Let me not forget the eternal dimension
  of the life Christ made possible.
For therein lies the secret
  of the power and the motive
    of meaningful living.
You've shown how true joy lies
  not in pampering oneself
  or in gratifying oneself
but in investing one's life
  in You and in others.

Lord, show me how to live my life
  Christ-style.

Make Me the Real Article

Lord, there's this problem of phoniness!

A lot of us have had
     some pretty high ideals,
  and we've respected the people
     who gave them to us.
Then they blew it all
  by not living up to
     what they preached.
Man, something like that
  can really turn you off in a hurry!

Why is it, Lord —
  that they can give you a lecture
     on not cheating in the classroom
  and then turn right around
     and cheat on an income-tax form?
  or warn against pot or LSD
     for your own health's sake
  and then go right out to a party
     and come home drunk?

30

or extol the virtues of honesty
   and sportsmanship in all things
and then chop someone down
   in a so-called shrewd deal?

And why is it that a church
   (that's what really bugs me —
      a church!)
can talk about
   "one God and Father of all,"
   "one Savior for all mankind,"
   "we are all one body in Christ,"
   and all such beautiful ideas
and then refuse to accept someone
   whose skin is a different hue,
   whose lifestyle has another flavor,
   whose ambitions aren't the same
as a friend and fellow member,
   a true brother or sister in Christ?

I tell You, Lord,
   there is a lot of phoniness around.
But then I guess You know this
   far better than I.
But what does it mean?
   That most people are hypocrites?
To be real honest,
I don't think so.

You did tell us (didn't You, Father?)
   that there is no such thing as
a man so perfect on this earth
   that he does only good
      and never sins.
And You also explained
   that's why You sent Jesus to earth.
Nobody's perfect.
   Everybody needs forgiveness.
Everybody needs that saving love
   wherein Christ gave Himself for us.

So I guess instead of picking off
   every little scab I can find on others
      and making an open sore,
I'd do better to chalk it up
   to the soul sickness in all of us
and pray that Your healing
   may be the final word.

Don't let me slip into the rut of those
   who feel smugly superior
because they sin openly,
   without pretense or shame.
They're not hypocritical, they say.
   They're being 100% honest.
   Theirs is the greatest virtue.

Somehow it seems to me such a smugness
  is the greatest hypocrisy of all.

I can respect someone
  who strives to live by high principle
    and fails.
But I cannot truly respect anyone
  who has no principles at all.

Father, give me
  conviction and principle
    high enough to be worth having.
Give me earnestness to live by them,
  and help me to do so.
I know there will be times
  when I slip,
  when I disappointingly fail.
But even then, Lord,
  make and keep me
    the real article.

About Teachers

I guess I've done
  more thinking and talking
    about teachers
than I ever did before, Lord.

When you're exposed to so many mentors,
you can't help
  making comparisons,
  choosing your favorites,
and making a mental note
  of the ones you want to avoid.

There's no problem in that.
  It's perfectly natural.
Perhaps it's good too
  that we thus learn
    to make wise selection.
But I fear I need a little help—
  actually we all do!—
when it comes to our attitudes
  about our different profs.

Take those we don't like, for example.
Some of them may be
    the greatest brains on campus
and may represent the highest
    in principles and ideals.

But because they have eccentricities
    in classroom manner
or are actually better researchers
    than face-to-face teachers,
we tend to brush them aside disdainfully
    and treat them with lack of respect.

Lord, don't let us do that!
Make us mature and wise enough
    to see them for what they are
and to give them
    the respect and courtesy they deserve.

And as for the ones we like,
    we often let our feelings go too far.
We tend to idolize them,
    and that's never good.

I know there has been only one Teacher
    that ever deserved to be worshiped.
In His case it isn't "idolizing,"
    for He was and is truly God.

Not only did Jesus command respect
   because His teachings were true
and because He could convey that truth
   right to the heart of man
but also because He was Truth
   right in Himself,
eternal Truth
   and infinite Love.
Yes, Him we worship and respect
   without reservation or apology.
We accept Him
   for what He was —
      and is.

Now, Lord, make us consistent in this
   so far as others are concerned.
Help us respect our teachers
   for what they truly are,
      not for what they are not.

Just because someone
      is sharp in his subject
   and really knows
      how to put it across
does not necessarily mean
   he holds the key
      to all the mysteries of life.

Many a prof has seen
   very little of life
      other than in his field
and has never lived
   in an atmosphere
      other than the academic.
There's no discredit in that.

But let me then accept him as authority
   where he is authority
      and not where he is not.
Most of all, don't let my admiration
   of others' mental prowess
turn me against You, Lord,
   because they have no room for You
      in their lives.
Their minds have limitations too.

Let me not confuse their horizons
   as the boundaries of life.

Let me never stop using Your truth
   as the touchstone to determine
what is ultimately valid
   and right.

About My Parents

Lord, there are some around here
  who never write home
    unless they need money,
who hardly bother to read
  letters from their parents.

"Who needs to read them?" they say.
"It will be the same thing
  they wrote last time
  and the time before that —
    'Don't do this!'
    'Don't do that!' —
preach, preach, preach
  from beginning to end!"

It's rather frightening
  to see how many
    have such attitudes.
They think only of themselves.
Other people, even parents,
  are there to be used.

We all grew up
    in basically the same way.
All through our little-kid years
    we were taking,
        taking all the time.
We were taking
    because they were lovingly giving.

Surely we should have
    grown up enough by now
    to recognize that
        their greatest gift
was their giving love,
    not what they gave in itself.
By now we should be appreciating
    them and their love
and not view them
    in terms of what we
        can still get out of them.

Lord, I do thank you for my parents —
    parents who could give
        without giving in,
    who could say no
        as well as yes,
    who recognized the importance
        of training their children.

I've always appreciated
   the good times we had together
and the way they anticipated
   my needs and desires.
But now I am most of all grateful
   for the intangibles.

These are their greatest gifts —
   their willingness to stand by me
      when I let them down;
   their readiness to forgive
      my inexcusable tantrums;
   the principles and values
      they implanted in me;
   their concern in leading me
      to You and Your love.

I appreciate too that,
      though I'm out of sight,
   I'm not out of their minds
      or out of their love.
Oh, it's true that I rather enjoy
   the feel of independence.
Learning to stand on my own two feet
   and to make my own decisions
is essential to maturity
   and preparing to meet the world.

But it's a rather nice feeling to know
    my folks' concerns and prayers
        are with me all the time
and that they're as close
        as a postage stamp
    when it comes to helping me out.

You too, never any farther
    than a prayer away,
. standing by me
    with infinite and unfailing love.
That love whereby You
    provided such a wonderful home
        and family for me,
    guided me safely on the path
        to a promising future,
    sent Christ to secure for me
        an eternally blessed future,
    filled my life
        with faith and hope.

Heavenly Father, don't ever let me
    get to feeling so big
that I no longer sense
    need for my family and You,
    appreciation of my family and You,
    love for my family and You.

42

And make me mature enough
   to recognize the importance
of not keeping these feelings to myself
   but of letting them in on them.

You can see right into
   my heart and mind.
They can't.
You can see the sincerity of my love.
Keep me mindful
   that I must show it to them.

About Faith

Heavenly Father, I've never seen You,
  yet I believe in You.

Ever since I was first pointed to You
  and made aware of my need of Jesus,
it seemed pretty natural
  to accept it all as true.
I still find hope and joy
  in knowing Jesus' great love for me.
None other was willing to die
  that I might live.

But strange things
  are happening, Father.
Sometimes lately
  I wonder about it all.
There are times when I feel
  uncomfortable,
  even embarrassed,
  almost even apologetic
about my faith.

I guess it's because others
   have been challenging my faith,
      even faith in general.
"The age of faith is gone," they say.
   "This is the age of reason,
      the age of science."

But really that's not at all true.
It hits me that in every field,
   even in the sciences,
sooner or later we reach the point
   where we deal with assumption.
We have gone beyond
   what can be tangibly proven
      or demonstrated.
Accepting anything beyond that point
   is a kind of faith,
      isn't it?

So why should I be embarrassed
   about my faith in You?
If some choose to base
   their present and future
on what Darwin said
   or Freud
or any other human being,
   I suppose that's their privilege.

I know I have a lot more going for me
    by holding on to You
and what You said and did
    and what You promised.

What I'm really asking for
    is a stronger faith.
Don't let me be influenced
    by those who delight in making
        a believing Christian squirm.
Keep me strong enough
    so that I not only
        love and trust my Savior
but also confess Him openly
    by being recognizably
        and consistently Christian.

Hand-Me-Downs

While I'm still thinking about faith,
  I might say, Father,
that I think I can even see some good
  in being put on the spot
    because of my faith.

Do You know why?
  (I guess that's a silly question!
    Of course You do!)
It forces me to think,
  to reevaluate and reappraise.
And that's always good.

When I was little, I used to get
  a lot of hand-me-downs.
They were good.
  I really didn't mind.
In fact, it gave me the thrill
  of knowing I was growing up.
I fit into the clothing
  of someone bigger.

As I look back, I have the feeling
   it was somewhat like that
      with my faith too.
It was more or less a hand-me-down.
I know Your Spirit
   was working in my heart,
and I have been happy
   in my faith.
I know too that there's nothing wrong
   in wearing what's passed on —
not when it's really good.
   And this is!

But, You know, I've reached a time
   when there is great joy in having
      something that is truly mine.
It's no longer good enough
   to believe something
just because others
   hold it to be true.
I have to find
   the joy and strength
      of personal conviction.

So really some of these attacks
   and challenges to my faith
may be serving a good purpose.

49

I'm not so stupid that,
    when others make snide remarks
        about my hand-me-downs,
I'd just shuck them off
    and run around spiritually naked.

Nor would I walk around in a space suit
    just so I could say:
"See, this is mine!
    It is representative of our age!
You'd better believe I did not get this
    from an older generation!"

Nor would I trade in my good clothes
    for the threadbare and dirty
just because a lot of others
    are going around that way.

Lord, I don't want to believe something
    just because my parents believed it.
But I don't want to disbelieve it either
    just because my parents believed it.

Help me find my way into Your Word.
    Lead me to the answers I need.
Show me Your unfailing Truth,
    so my faith can be strong,
personally and meaningfully mine.

Then, when others challenge,
   I won't be thrown for a loss.
Empowered by Your Spirit,
   I'll be able to say:
"I know what I believe!
   And in whom I believe!"
      And that's that!

Friends

"No man is an island,"
   I've often heard it said.
I'm sure it's true, Lord.
   Everyone needs friends.
No one can be completely happy
   going it all alone.

Even You, Lord Jesus,
   carefully selected companions
to share Your days,
   Your plans,
   Your mission.

What disappointment You felt when,
   in Your worst hours,
You had to pray alone,
   stand alone,
   and die alone!
For the rest, even Your friends,
   did not understand
      what was really going on.

I know, Lord, how important
   the right kind of friends can be.
Picking a friend requires greater care
   than selecting courses
   or choosing books.
For after books have been discarded
   and courses dropped or completed,
friends will still
   be exerting influence,
      be it good or bad.
Either that,
   or they will let you down
      when you need them most.

I know this sounds so simple,
   so completely logical.
I should let my ideals
   determine my friends
rather than my friends
   determine my ideals.
But I'm aware also
   of my readiness to settle
      for second best.

So I'm turning to You, Lord,
   asking You to help me
   find the right friends.

I'm turning to You,
    for You have shown Yourself
to be "the Friend
    that sticks closer than a brother,"
the Friend who gave His life
    for His friends.

My true Friend, guide me
    to such companions
as will stand by me
    and strengthen me always,
who will gladly share my sorrows
    as well as my joys.
And make me such a friend
    to them.

I Believe in One God

In days past I had little difficulty
   in coming to You, Father,
as a trusting child comes
   to a loving father.

Now it is insinuated that I am
   unrealistic,
   naive,
   irrational.
Why the Father image? some ask.
   Why even a personal God?
Isn't it enough to concede
   there is "That Whatever"
   that pervades the universe?
Enough to merely align
   or at least attune oneself
   to that realization?

I know some live by that principle,
   live even more altruistically
than many who boast truer religion.

But then I come back to this—
   such neither proves You
   nor disproves You.
It is no reflection on Your Being.
It only reflects on us,
   who bear Your name
   and claim Your lordship.

What others claim
   or disclaim about You
determines neither Your essence
   nor Your character.
God is not made!
Much less is He made
   in the image of man
   or by the mind of man.
It's the other way around:
   You are the Creator of all,
   we just a part of Your creation.

If there are those who judge You
   less than You really are,
   perhaps we are to blame.
Perhaps, as they say,
   we've given the impression
that our faith is that
   of a "God-in-the-box."

As if we were securely content
   just to have You around
and take a reassuring peek
   every once in a while
and know that when we press
   the panic button
You will spring to our service
   and all will be well.

Father, to whatever extent
   I have treated You
as a spiritual convenience,
   please forgive me!

And forgive the hurt
   I have done others
who formed their spiritual opinions
   by what they saw in me.

Let me not compound error
   by going still farther
in elevating myself
   and abasing You.

That's what I would be doing
   if I were to give in
to some of the popular ideas
   about an impersonal God.

Sometimes they can make it sound
  so scientific,
  so learned,
  so logical,
  so plausible.
But isn't it still just a basic
  and unvarnished denial?
Isn't it just another glib attempt
  to dethrone You from men's hearts?

Father, I thank You —
for having revealed Yourself
  as more than nondescript reality,
for having manifested Your power
and offering Your love
  in more than the wonders of nature,
for showing Yourself as One
  who is above all and in all,
  who has mind and will,
  who is eternal and almighty.

I thank You also for revealing
  what our minds cannot comprehend —
the mystery of Your being one God,
  yet Father, Son, and Holy Spirit.
Others may stub their toes on this,
  but I rejoice in it.

As You go beyond
   our ability to fathom,
as You stagger our imagination
   and defy rational analysis,
You most declare Yourself as God.

Therein lies our fullest hope —
   Your wisdom is greater
      than our understanding,
   Your might greater
      than our powers,
   Your love greater
      than our affections.
That's the whole point,
   the glory of it all —
You stand alone above all else,
   the one God.

I thank You also
   for revealing Yourself as the One
      who really cares,
      who watches and guides,
      who is concerned about us.
I thank You that Your love
   is as unending as You are,
that Your concern for us extends
   even beyond our earthly limits.

I thank You for sending
    Your beloved Son
to seek and effect our eternal good
    through His personal self-sacrifice.
I thank You for accepting us
    as Your children
and giving us the right
    to see You as our Father.

For one can fear a Reality
    and respect a Being,
but one loves a Father
    who is all Love in Himself.

Give me such unqualified love
    for You, Father.
If others still choose
    to mold their own gods,
let it not be because of me.

I Feel a Bit Down, Lord!

Father, sometimes I feel so out of it,
   so depressed,
   so empty,
I wonder if I can go on
   or if it's even worth it.
If I didn't have You,
   I don't know what I'd do.

There are days
   when nothing makes sense.
I don't know which way to turn,
   which door to open.
Each door I try
   seems to lead nowhere.
It's like walking
   into one dark, cluttered closet
   after another.

 O Father, send me light,
   guidance,
   direction.

61

Peel off my spiritual cataracts
    that life may be more than blur.
Let me see You clearly
    before me,
inviting me to walk with You
    on the way,
where every step
    is glorious adventure
and the destination
    the greatest joy of all.

Father, one thing more!
It's mostly when I'm all alone
    I get these empty feelings
and I almost drown
    in self-pity.

I want to cry out:
"Doesn't anybody know me well enough
    to sense my needs?
Doesn't anybody care?"

I guess what I'm asking for
    is a touch that I can feel,
a hand, a shoulder,
    tangible and reassuring.
Please, Lord, send someone to fill
    the vacuum in my heart!

What About Jesus?

"What do you think of Jesus?"

Jesus Himself asked that question
   of the people of His day.
Twenty centuries later
   we're still answering.
But I'm sure You're not too happy
   with some of our answers, Father.

I'm afraid it often amounts to
   little more than:
      "Not very much!"
It's not that we want to say that.
It's just that we let other things
   crowd Him out of our mind
      and out of our life.
Sometimes it ends up
   that our mind is like
      a cluttered psychedelic shop
where the picture of Jesus
   is lost somewhere

between film stars and monsters,
between the op art posters
    and the Campbell Soup labels.
But why?

Why such a flutter of excitement
    when an unknown little guru
pops out of some far cave or cloister,
    speaking vague generalities
        of life and love,
        of finding oneself?

Why, when we tend to relegate Jesus
    to an unopened book
and bypass Him uninterestedly
    as if He had nothing to offer?

Reminds me of a fellow who has it made
    with the most beautiful
        and wonderful girl in the world,
then chases every skirt that walks by.
Why?
And why, in this enlightened age,
    the sudden resurgence
and curious obsession with superstitions
    of the occult,
    of Satanism,
    of astrological claptrap?

65

Dare I or anyone concede
    that this is Satan's day?
And live as though "he's got
    the whole world in his hands"?
Has Christ become the Unnecessary?
    the Hope of yesterday?

"What do you think of Jesus?"
Father, I hope my attitudes
    and actions reveal
that I think a great deal of Jesus
    and that I really know Him.

Not just that I know a lot about Him,
    but that I really know Him—
        and believe Him
        and trust Him
without reservation or apology.

Certainly we can see Him
    to be more vibrantly alive
than any of the little prophets
    who momentarily make
        headlines today.

Certainly what He said
    and what He did

supersedes all that others
  have claimed and offered.
Certainly the fine-tooth-combing
  and critical scrutiny of years
has substantiated His truth
  and His perfectness.

As we in the "now" world
  weigh His claims
and witness His life,
  His sacrificial death,
  His triumphant new life,
how can we help exclaiming,
  as did the soldier on Calvary,
"Truly this is the Son of God!"

Father, do not let me be content
  to regard Jesus
    as only a great teacher.
Let Him never be less to me
  than my best Friend,
  my eternal Savior,
  my unfailing Strength,
  my undying Hope.
And let what Jesus means to me
  always show through.

Where's the Action?

Father, sometimes I get so restless.
I seldom enjoy
    just sitting and thinking.
I like to be doing something!
    I want action!
Maybe that's characteristic of my age.

But, Father, I don't want
    to get caught up
        in today's nervous twitch.
I have enough sense
    to know that frenetic movement
is not the kind of action
    that brings satisfaction.
It only leaves a person tired
    and disappointed.

I want to do,
    but I also want
to see point and worth
    in what I do.

I'm fed up with people who talk
   about justice,
   equal opportunity for all,
   nondiscrimination,
   love and brotherhood,
and do nothing about it.
Not only do they back off
   so they don't get involved.
They don't even practice it personally
   in their thinking and living.

I know You understand, Father.
Because when I read Your Word
   and think about it,
I see You didn't stop with words
   that tell of Your love for us
   in an abstract way.
You go on to show that love
   in terms of action.
It's what You did for us all,
   even more than what You said,
that makes it clear to me
   what love and life are all about.

Sending Your very own Son to save us.
That's action!
   It tells more than words!

Jesus' whole unselfcentered life,
    His serving even by dying,
to gain peace
    and unending hope for us
is the most significant action of all.

And Christ's breakthrough from death!
Not ideas about immortality
    but the action of victory —
that's reason for faith!

So I guess I'm really not
    out in left field
        when I have the itch
        to see things happen.
But, Father, give me enough wisdom
    to think things through
    and pray things through first.

If I'm going to spend my time
    and energy in something,
I'd like it to be worthwhile.
I'd like to know I'm doing
    the right thing in the right way.

And, Father, somehow I'd like
    love to show through my actions
        the way it does through Yours.

Love and Peace

Lord Jesus, how often I've heard—
  and the song is never out of date—
"What the world needs most
  is love, sweet love,
No, not just for some but for everyone."

Yet while we yearn for love
  and long for lasting peace,
what can we do to attain it?
  And keep it?

Obviously, carrying placards
  won't assure these blessings
any more than complaining about prices
  will lick inflation.

We need fewer demonstrations
  for love and peace
and more demonstrations
  of love and peace.

And, Lord Jesus, that's where You come in!

There was no confusion in Your mind
  as to what love is — or peace.
Nor was there anything unclear
  as to how to live that love.
You did not lecture others.
  You Yourself set
    the perfect example of love.
You are Love!
  You are the Prince of Peace!

I often wonder how
  You could know such love.
Oh, I don't mean how You could
  heal the sick,
  strengthen the weak,
  or raise the fallen.
There are vestiges of such compassion
  in all of us,
even though we lack the ability
  to do much about it.

But why You would choose
  to undertake the mission
of saving people who are hell-bent
  on self-destructing —
this kind of love
  I find hard to understand.

Yet love brought You
  into this world.
Love placed You
  in the middle
    of our civilized unloveliness.
Love caused You to live and die —
  not just with us
  but for us.

"Christ died for us
  while we were yet sinners."
I cannot but marvel
  at those words
and joyously accept
  the love that made such sacrifice.

All this —
  and heaven too!
Lord Jesus, let me never belittle
  all You made possible for us.
"He that believes
  shall have everlasting life" —
this is the ultimate blessing
  of Your love.
So through Your love
  I can also know
  and understand peace.

Conflict may threaten
  and disturbance disrupt.
But by Your love
  I know a peace
    that surpasses all —
a peace with God
  and potential peace with others.
Some in this world
  may not understand it
    or think it possible.
But I know it, Jesus,
  because You've promised it
    and You've given it.

I thank You for it,
  and I pray that somehow
Your love and Your peace
  may be passed on through me
    to others —
to both the lovelies
  and the unlovelies
of this world.

Freedom!

"Born free!"
What a wonderful sound!

"Land of the free!"
"Sweet land of liberty" —
what a wonderful thought!

Freedom!

All my life I've been singing
    about freedom.
But until recently I never stopped
    to ask what it really means.

Oh, I don't mean
    national independence
or prohibition of slavery
    or citizens' rights.
I mean about
    freedom and me.
How free am I?
    What actually is freedom?

Since I've entered college
  and have enjoyed
my first real taste of independence,
  I've been told:
"You're free, man!
  Really free!
That means you do what you want!
  You're your own boss!
You're on your own!"

It sounds good—
  maybe deceivingly so.
Somewhere there has to be a limit.
  Isn't that true, Father?

Somehow I recall these words:
  "Live as free men,
yet without using your freedom
  as a pretext for evil."
As is always the case with Your Word,
  that's the best I've ever read
    on this subject.

Live free—
  but don't misuse your freedom.
That puts the burden on me,
  doesn't it, Father?

In enjoying my freedom
  I do not have the right
    to do wrong,
    to hurt another.
Yet I'm free —
  really free!

That's what seems to be ignored
  in some of the current bids
    for freedom.
Like that free-speech thing
  awhile back.
Free speech is one thing.
  But to demand the right
to smear their mental excrement
    so publicly
  that others cannot avoid it —
    that's something quite different.
Yet that's what happens
  over and over again.

I'm not belittling
    one's rights
  or the exercise
    of one's freedom.
A person should stand up
  for what he believes.

But stooping to violence
   and wanton vandalism,
trying to bait and provoke
   by flagrant breaking of the law—
how can anyone justify
   such bids for attention?
I don't care how worthy the cause
   or how intense the dissent,
it just can't lead to that.

I'm not saying this
   because I'm talking to You, Father,
and I think it the proper thing to say
   under the circumstance.
It's just that this is not consistent
   with the ideal of true freedom.

Lord, I'm truly grateful
   for the privilege of
      being born free
      and living free.
I know some do not enjoy
   the same measure of freedom.
Let me live my freedom responsibly,
   for others' good as well as my own.
Help me stand up for what is right,
   but let me do it in a proper way.

The Real Me

It was Robert Burns —
  wasn't it, Lord? —
who wished we had the power
  to see ourselves as others see us.
I sometimes think about
  being in others' shoes
and seeing myself
  coldly and objectively.
How different would I seem?

I can't say I get too concerned
  about it though.
For much of the time others see us
  the way we want them to.

What matters more
  is how You see us, Lord.
There is far more sense
  in my wishing and praying
for the power to see myself
  through Your eyes.

Then I would be seeing
   the real me.
For You are the One
   who penetrates past
all pretense and illusion,
   all the formality of cover-up.

I suppose that,
   had I that point of vantage,
I'd pay less attention
   to my daily happenings
      and more to my attitudes,
less to my actions,
   more to my reasons for doing.

"Had I that point of vantage" —
   is that what I really said, Lord?
Father, I know better!
   I know You mirrored us
      in Your Word.
All I have to do
      is look in it,
   and I can see myself clearly.
Maybe that's the trouble
      with many of us;
   maybe we don't really
      want to see.

Like this word "sinner."
   You label us all that way.
It's neither pretty nor pleasant
   to think of us as such.
Some of these new religions
   have a lot more appeal
when they stress the inherent goodness
   of all mankind
and explain away sin as weakness
   that can be easily overlooked
   and eventually overcome.
After all, nobody likes to feel guilty.

But then it wasn't your aim
   to make us live
with a burden of guilt —
   was it, Lord?
Any more than when a doctor
   tells a sick person he's sick.

If that's what You wanted —
   just to accuse us of being sinful —
You'd have told us
   where to go.
You'd have scratched us off
   as no-goods,
   as worthless nobodies.

But You didn't.
Instead You emphasized our worth.
You proved how highly You rate us
  by paying the highest price possible
  for our eternal good.
You didn't just pinpoint the disease.
  You sent the Cure.
Jesus by His self-sacrifice
  brought life in place of death,
forgiveness in place of guilt,
  hope in place of despair.
That's what it all means.
  Right, Father?

Maybe I will still have to go on
  seeing myself a sinner
but, thanks to You,
  a forgiven one.
Maybe I will still see myself
  much in need of help,
but, thanks to You,
  I see my eternal Help.

Secret Agent 00-0

What's the matter with me, Father?
  You've never disowned me.
Even in my worst moments,
  when I'd have been ashamed
to be seen by anyone I love,
  You've seen me.
Yet You were still willing
  to claim me as Your very own.
You even went so far
  as to send Your own beloved Son
to make and keep me a part
  of Your eternal family.

Yet there are times when,
  by all outward signs,
    I am disowning You.
Ashamed of You?
  How could I possibly be?

Why then do I tend so often
  to cover up my Christian faith?

Why do I hesitate
  to hang a cross on my wall
    or a picture of Jesus?
Why do I put Bible and prayer book
  where they are inconspicuous?
Is it that I am ashamed of You?
Or that I do not have
  the courage to be myself
    with my present friends?
Am I in the wrong crowd?

Help me see, Father,
  that life and faith
    are not games we play.
I know what Jesus said about
  letting light shine,
    not hiding the lamp under a bushel,
    shouting from the housetops.

I know too that Jesus went through
  far more for me
than I would ever have to go through
  for Him,
even if everyone else would turn
  against me,
because of my readiness to be
  recognized and counted a Christian.

In God's kingdom there is no need
  for a Christian undercover man.
The secret agent there
  might as well be assigned
the number Double-O-Zero,
  because that's all he's worth —
    nothing!

I know this,
  and I believe it true.
Now give me the courage
  to live my faith openly.

By that I mean more than sporting
  decal fish symbols
or bumper stickers like
  "Honk if you love Jesus."

Father, help me to live my faith that
  everything I say,
  everything I do
may be positive public confession
  that Jesus lives in me,
  and I live in Him.

Midterm Jitters

It's that time again, Father,
  panic-and-black-coffee time!
So much is hanging in the balance.
  The pressure is really on.

I know it would be easier if I
  had prepared more conscientiously
    from day to day.
But there's little to do about it now.

I ask, Father, that You keep me
  coolheaded and alert.
Don't let fatigue
  or nervousness
keep me from doing the best possible
  both in preparing
  and on the exam.

And keep me honest, Father.

Don't let me succumb
  to the temptation to cheat.

If I have goofed off so badly all year
that I can't make it on my own,
    then I deserve to fail.
I wouldn't go very far in life
    if I tried to hitchhike all the way.
Sooner or later I have to learn
    to stand on my own feet,
    to make my own way.
It's better I learn this now,
    hard as it might be,
and to learn the worth of honesty.
So it's off to last-minute cramming!
Father, help me do my best.

All through life, Father!
I know my ultimate salvation
    lies in Your grace,
    in Christ's love.
I'm also aware that my whole life
    shows what this means to me.

I know already now that someday
    there will be a final exam
    when I will stand before You.
Don't let me make the tragic mistake
    of putting off till then
    what I should be doing now.

Conformity

Lord Jesus, in this day of multicopy
   and mass production
we are caught in the dilemma
   of conformity versus nonconformity.

Lord, I don't want to be
   a conformist.
There's enough carbon-copyishness
   in the establishment today.
There's room for fresh thinking,
   need for originality.

But Lord, I don't want to be
   a nonconformist either —
that is, a deliberate nonconformist
   who takes delight
      in being different
   just for the sake
      of being different.
There is enough madness
   already in this world.

Anyway, Lord, there are so many
  who boast of nonconformity
who are the worst offenders
  in this line themselves.
They're all alike —
  just another mindless mass
  with a new look.
It reminds me of a herd
  of Hereford steers
laughing at and condemning
  a flock of sheep
because they look alike
  and bleat alike.
Change the color,
  and substitute a "moo,"
but what's the difference?

Lord, show me how to be myself,
  to do my own thinking.
When this calls for being different —
  well, then, let me be different.
When not, let me not be embarrassed
  for being like others.

Help me conform to Your pattern.
You stood alone, Lord Jesus,
  so different from the rest.

But dress or appearance
  had nothing to do with it.
Such inconsequentials
  as styles and fads never do.

The difference lay
  in who You were.
  in Your purpose in life,
    in Your unyielding truth.
You never ceased being Your true Self,
  though many hated You for it.
You never swerved from Your mission
  of reconciling man to God,
though both world and church
  threw obstacles in Your way.

Lord Jesus, make me more like You!

Yes, I have the same desire
  as everyone else —
    to be accepted,
    to be "in" with the group.
But, Lord, I want above all
  to be "in" with You.
If there be conformity,
  let it be to Your mind
    and Your ways.

The Sex Binge

I read somewhere, Father,
  that other countries in the world
are amazed and confused
  at our American preoccupation
    and obsession with sex.

It is said we must be coming of age—
  that this is a long overdue,
though unfortunately exaggerated,
  emergence from Puritan beginnings,
an overthrow of Victorian traditions.

Call it what they will,
  I know we are
  in the middle
    of a big sex binge.
Sex themes saturate
  movies and TV,
  books and magazines,
  fashions and advertising,
  humor and conversation.

Some say this is healthy —
that there's less harm in the open
  than in the suggestive,
less in the completely exposed
  that in the filmy and see-through.

I'm not so sure about either way.
  A lot depends on circumstances.
If I were in the Peace Corps,
  serving where the locals
    run around in the nude,
I'd consider this normal
  and possibly also healthy.
But it's a little different here,
  where exposure and semiexposure
are intended to arouse and excite.

That's the sick part in our situation:
  Sex is being exploited.
They can talk all they want to
  about being realistic,
    sophisticated,
    adult,
    mature,
    continental,
they're still pandering sex
  in a cheap and dirty way.

94

I don't think I'm being prudish,
  am I, Father?
I look on the human body
  as being truly beautiful.
To think otherwise would be
  to belittle Your creation.
But I think there's a time and place
  for that beauty to be enjoyed,
and that's not on public display.

I consider the acts of love
  beautiful too —
in fact, the whole concept
  of love and marriage.
But don't good taste
  and common decency
impose certain limits
  on how much of these acts
  or their perversions
should be spelled out in print
  or shown on the screen?

I know that we young
  have a natural curiosity —
  some say "a prurient interest."
I know we are very vulnerable
  to this kind of temptation.

But do You know what gets me, Father?
They talk about "youthful lusts,"
  but it's the older people
who write and publish most pornography,
  who film questionable pictures
and run topless shows
and design provocative styles.

We didn't ask for them.
  We don't particularly want them.
What are we supposed to do?
  Stop going to shows?
  Quit reading fiction?
  Just stick to blue jeans?

Oh, I know I can't
    blame it all
on the dirty old men
    in this world.
If there weren't
    a lot of money in it,
  they'd go into
    a different business
  or at least change direction.
And they claim that
  most of their income
    comes from the youth.

So it comes back to us again.
Father, help me
   accept the responsibility
      of keeping myself clean.
"A clean heart
   and a pure mind" —
some people may call that corny,
   but I know that's the only way
to the healthy attitude
   so necessary
      to a lastingly happy life.

New Morality?

I guess it isn't really,
    is it, Father?
It's neither really "new,"
    nor is it particularly "moral."

I've heard preachers denounce it,
    saying "the new morality
    is the same old immorality."
Sometimes then I feel like crying out,
    "You're probably right.
But can't we talk about it?
    We do have problems.
    We do need answers."

There's this strong feeling
    among so many my age
that we have to relax our code
    and conform standards to our needs.
This doesn't mean
    we do not want to be moral
    or do not want to live responsibly.

It's just that present-day demands
   are a little different.
We mature
   and are biologically
      ready for marriage
at the same age
   as our ancestors
      through the ages.
But the current need for advanced
   and specialized education
keeps getting in the way.

You can almost understand
   why we sometimes feel frustrated
and want to claim the right
   to enjoy the fuller tastes of love
      before we are married.

I don't mean we want
   to be promiscuous.
I know there are many
   who have little regard for morality,
who wallow in promiscuity
   and boast of their conquests.
I'm not thinking of them.
What about us who really love
   and do not want to wait?

It's not like it was with Joseph,
  who fled plain seduction,
  unvarnished adultery,
protesting that he could not
  do this great wickedness
  and sin against God.

What about when you really do
  love someone very much
and feel it unfair
  to have to postpone
the gratification of love
  who knows how long?

What's the answer, Father?
Living together?
  My parents would really scream!
But they don't have to worry.
  That wouldn't be my choice anyway.

I don't see that that fits
  Your beautiful plan of love.
You made man and woman
  to complement each other,
  to fulfill each other.
"The two shall be one," You said,
  and Jesus added,

"Man must not separate, then,
     what God has joined together."

That's the way I see
     the love I'm looking for.
I want to be one of two—
     in all of life,
     for all of life.

I see real love as an epoxy,
     a binding, lasting commitment.
If it's primarily self-seeking
     and momentarily self-fulfilling
it's not really love.
Love gives!
When two love
     they live for each other.
They see it as a permanent oneness,
     not a temporary arrangement.

That's why I can't see
     living together as the answer.
It smacks too much of sex
     and not enough of love.
It's too much the old routine of
     "try it, you'll like it,"
and if you don't like it
     you can just walk away from it.

No thanks, Lord!
  . That's not enough for me!

Oh, I know the classic arguments
    against marriage
    or any form of commitment.
They say their relationship
    is more meaningful
just because there are no strings attached,
    no marriage license,
    no vows or promises.
Make no promise,
    break no promise.

But that kind of relationship
    I don't want.
When I give myself in love
    I want to give myself completely,
without reservation
    or fine print escape clause.
And I'm looking for a return
    of that same kind of love—
where we can enjoy sex
    as channel and vehicle
        of self-giving;
where respect and trust
    are coupled with love.

So help me, Father!
  I know what I want,
and my strong feelings tell me
  I want it now.

But if I'm not really ready,
  give me the sense
to pray for an override
  on today's impatience.

I'd like my future years
  to be years of unsullied happiness,
    not of lingering regrets.
I know that if I make serious effort
  to follow Your blueprints
    of love and marriage,
I can end up with a happy home
  and a wonderful family—
not with what's next best.

The Pill

One short afterthought, Father.
It has to do with the pill,
   heralded by some
as the greatest thing to hit the campus
   since coeducation.

I realize this doesn't change anything
   so far as morals are concerned.
It only points up the need
   for greater personal moral strength.

If fear of pregnancy
   was the prime reason
why some did not play
   fast and loose,
they had a pretty shaky foundation
   from the very beginning.
So I suppose the pill
   in its own small way
helps show up a person's
   true colors.

I know it heightens temptation.
In these years of learning
   there is often strong desire
to pile up experiences,
   to taste something new.

There is the tendency
   to justify.
There is the tendency
   to reason:
"Why not?
   When no one gets hurt?"

That's the deception of it all,
   the illusion that
      "no one gets hurt."
Is pregnancy
   the only form of hurt?
Aren't we getting hurt
   every time we succumb
      to temptation?
   every time we go against
      our conscience?
   every time we go counter
      to Your ways?
And aren't we hurting others
   at the same time?

Father, I sense Your wisdom again
    in every step
        of scientific progress —
    yes, even in this pill.
But not just from
    the physiological standpoint.
It's things like this
    that give us the chance to show
we are moral by choice,
    not by default.

Grass, Booze, and Other Junk

There's surely much
  confused thinking
about this whole matter
  of drugs and drink, Lord.
There are an awful lot of people
  who could take
    a little straightening out.
I don't just mean kids, Lord.
  Some on the other side
    of the fence too.

I know, and so does everybody else,
  that there's a lot
    of the junk around
    and a lot being used.
I could have laid my hands on it
  already back in junior high.
Certainly it's easier now.

But I resent it when older people
  look down their noses

at all of us our age
   as if we were potheads.
And I don't like being classified
   as "The Hooked Generation."

Maybe I'm being oversensitive.
Maybe I should be more appreciative
   of their concern
   for our total well-being—
though I could take it more seriously
   if they weren't so turned on
   to alcohol and tobacco.

Lord, I'm not belittling the problem.
   There is a lot of temptation,
and there are a lot of unfortunates
   who have become addicted,
even though they were confident
   they'd never get hooked.

But I've read and seen so much
   about H and grass and acid,
about immediate and accumulative effect,
   about the pain of kicking the habit.
And I'm sick of arguments
   on legalizing mary jane,
   or whether it's really addictive,

even as I'm sick of hearing
   of those who've experimented.
Strange sights,
   expanded sensations,
weird new dimensions
   of sound and color—
who cares?
   Life is tough enough
without risking a bad trip
   into Psychedelialand.

That's the way I'm getting to feel
   about booze and cigarettes too.
What difference does it make
   if it's legal or not?
What good is anything—
   if it blows your mind?
   if it damages your liver?
   if it leads to lung cancer?
Who needs those kinds of crutches?
   Who wants them?

Lord, I don't want to run through life
   looking for illusive escape,
and I don't want to take a chance
   of committing partial suicide
for the sake of a few party thrills
   or cheap new sensations.

You have given us healthy bodies
   and healthy minds, Lord.
We have most of our lives still ahead,
   and potentially healthy futures.
It's a great, big, wonderful world
   You've given us.
Make and keep us wise enough
   to enjoy it in good health.

The Rules of the Game

Father, there seems to be
    a real hangup
  in the "now" generation
over this whole business
  of rules and regulations.

There is constant tension
  between those who demand
    compliance with the rules
and those who refuse
  to comply with any rule
    they do not agree with.

It's an infringement
  on personal liberty,
    they claim,
and they insist the best way
  to show disapproval
    is to openly disobey it.
And so the tension mounts,
  and clashes occur.

I seem to be caught
  in a crossfire, Father.
I do question the rationale
  behind some of the rules.
But I also recognize the importance
  rules play in everything.

I remember what it was like
  back in my preteens.
We used to get a game going
  whenever we could get
    a bunch together.
Somehow the losers
  always wanted to change the rules.
After the third wild swing
  came the demand,
"Let's make it four strikes!"
And when the wrong side
  of the flipped coin appeared,
"How about two out of three?"
  "Three out of five?"
Likely as not, the game soon ended
  in chaos and bickering.

You can't play any game very long
  unless you have rules
    and stick to the rules.

I'm sure it's little different
   in the game of life.
There have to be rules,
   and they must be respected.
Yes, there will be infringement
   on someone's personal freedom,
the way some interpret freedom
   as the right to do
      absolutely anything.

The question is:
   Who draws up the rules?
For a starter, we all have to agree
   that You do, Father.
When it comes down
   to the very basics of life,
we must come back to the rules
   You gave us long ago.

I know there are some that disagree.
They say those were intended
   for another people
   of another culture
   and another day.
But I can't buy that.
Centuries after You first gave them,
   Christ reaffirmed them.

He did even more than that:
He lashed out —
   not only at those
     who ignored them
   but even at those
     who obeyed superficially.

These aren't just rules
   for when the umpire's looking.
These are the meat
   of life itself.
They require depth acceptance.

There's a lot that can be changed
   in the rules of daily living.
But not the ten basics.
   I can see that.
They're like the operator's manual
   the manufacturer gives
for the proper care and use
   of the new machine.
Follow it,
   and there's smooth sailing ahead.
Ignore it,
   and whose fault is it
     when everything goes wrong?

Second Thoughts on Rules

Father, I fear I sidetracked myself.
By zeroing in on Your law,
  which as a Christian
I can do nothing but accept
  as absolute authority,
I've left untouched
    the troublesome area
  of man-made rules
    and regulations.

That we need such rules
  is also obvious.
We've lived with them
  and profited by them
ever since our parents forbade us
  to run out into the street
and required us to wash
  before sitting down at the table.

Sometimes we resented such rules,
  but we needed them.

We needed them because
 we didn't have sense enough
 to do such things
 of our own accord.
The rules were patterned for our good,
 and like them or not,
they proved to be for our good
 as they were rigidly enforced.

Why then should we be taken aback
 at comparable regulations today?
Have I, or any of us, progressed
 to a state of such common sense
or accepted such responsibility
 and considerateness toward others
that we no longer need
authoritative standards?
I know good and well
 that if speed limits
 were not posted and enforced
we'd go barreling
 down the highway
 with little thought
 of consequence.

Yes, I admit
 we need rules and laws.

But rules do change,
   don't they, Father?
Some prove unreasonable.
Some are found to be unfair,
   prejudicial,
   discriminatory,
   way out of date.
If rules didn't change,
   we'd still be driving at 10 mph
and wearing swimsuits
   that went down to the knees.
Pitchers would still be
   throwing spitballs legally,
and supertall basketball players
   would be making dunk shots.
Rules have to be changed
   as they lose point and purpose.

But when, Father? And by whom?

Certainly I'm not referring
   to Your commandments, Father.
I do admit there are times
   I'm not sure of the why
      of Your directives.
And times when I regret
   their restriction.

But I know Yours is the final Word
    and that it always brings about
        what is truly best.

But these others,
    what about them?
When a law reflects
    the bigotry of man,
it must be changed,
    must it not, Father?
And if it is not,
    what then?
Must we not speak up
    and work to make it right?
Are we not our brothers' keepers?
Are we not to strive for the truth
    that brings freedom?
If we do not care enough,
    who will?

But, Father, I know better
    than to fight wrong
    by doing more wrong.
Nor do I believe
        one achieves good
        by bullying others around
        or by provoking authority.

I know the disciples
    disobeyed the demand
  that they stop preaching Christ.
In obedience to
    their Higher Authority
  they just kept on telling of Jesus.
But they did not taunt
  the local guard
or delight in stirring up trouble.
Nor did they,
  even in their open noncompliance,
disobey their Lord's command
  to be subject to,
  to honor and respect
    the higher powers.

"We must obey God rather than men."

Such must always be
  my final decision.
When it becomes necessary
  to take a stand,
    let it be for right.
Let it never reflect bare defiance
  or plain rebelliousness.
Let it not be a bold bid
  to have my own way.

Let it show that I am standing
   for something,
   not just against something.
Let me never become one
   of the unthinking mob
that permits itself to be used
   by contenders for dubious causes
   that can excite the empty mind.

When I stand, Father, let it be
   on my own personal conviction,
and make my conviction be
   in accord with Your will.

The End?

Whee!

It's over!
Thanks to You, Father,
    I made it!
The diploma in hand
    gives mute testimony
that I have completed
    all requirements
and am entitled
    to write
    a couple of letters
    behind my signature.

In a way
    I hate to see it end.
There have been so many
    happy days
    and warm friendships.
Most of these will become
    only pleasant memories.

But I shouldn't be
    looking back regretfully.
I should be thanking You
    for Your many obvious blessings
    all through these years.

It really is in joy
    that I leave school, Father.
It seems I've spent
    most of my life
    in a classroom
preparing,
    always preparing.
Now I have the chance
    to make the life
I've been preparing for.

I step forward boldly,
    yet with misgiving.
I know I don't have
    all the answers —
perhaps not even as many
    as I think I do.
Yet I step forward with courage,
    for I step in faith.
I have this confidence
    that You are with me.

As You guided and guarded me
   these years of college,
You will continue to help me
   in Your unfailing love.

I know I dare not
   view this as an end.
Commencement implies beginning;
graduation, moving up
   to a new level.
If my life is to be worthwhile,
   I will have to continue
growing and learning
   in all the years ahead.

So I begin again.
Bless me, Father!
Keep me conscious of Your presence,
   grateful for Your love,
   trusting in Your power.
Through Christ I am Yours.
   Keep me Yours
      now and always.